W9-AUD-524

DOGS SET VII

LABRADOODLES

Jill C. Wheeler
ABDO Publishing Company

visit us at
www.abdopublishing.com

Published by ABDO Publishing Company, 8000 West 78th Street, Edina, Minnesota 55439. Copyright © 2008 by Abdo Consulting Group, Inc. International copyrights reserved in all countries. No part of this book may be reproduced in any form without written permission from the publisher. The Checkerboard Library™ is a trademark and logo of ABDO Publishing Company.

Printed in the United States.

Cover Photo: Chelle Rohde Calbert/www.designerdoggies.com
Interior Photos: Chelle Rohde Calbert/www.designerdoggies.com pp. 13, 19;
    Corbis pp. 10, 14, 15, 17, 21; Getty Images pp. 5, 11; Heidi M.D. Elston p. 7;
    Peter Arnold p. 9

Editors: Heidi M.D. Elston, BreAnn Rumsch
Art Direction: Neil Klinepier

Library of Congress Cataloging-in-Publication Data

Wheeler, Jill C., 1964-
 Labradoodles / Jill C. Wheeler.
     p. cm. -- (Dogs. Set VII)
 Includes index.
 ISBN 978-1-59928-964-9
 1. Labradoodle--Juvenile literature. I. Title.

 SF429.L29W44 2008
 636.72--dc22

                        2007031508

CONTENTS

DESIGNING THE PERFECT POOCH

Dogs and humans have lived together for more than 12,000 years. Modern dogs are descendants of wolf pups tamed to help ancient peoples hunt. Dogs and wolves are part of the Canidae **family**.

Would-be dog owners have hundreds of dog **breeds** to choose from today. Yet, some people are still searching for the perfect dog. For many, the new answer is a designer dog.

A designer dog is created by crossing two different **purebreds**. This produces a dog that does not exactly match its mother's or father's genes. So the chances of eliminating an undesirable gene, such as the one that causes shedding, increase.

For this reason, many people believe designer dogs are healthier than **purebreds**. However, it is impossible to know which genes will be passed on.

Still, a designer dog might be just the dog someone is dreaming of. For Labradoodles, that is often the case. Labradoodles are a mix of Labrador retriever and poodle.

LABRADOR RETRIEVERS

Labrador retrievers came from Newfoundland in eastern Canada. The ancestors of today's Labrador retrievers were small dogs. They were good swimmers and helpful to hunters.

Those small dogs were crossed with large Newfoundland dogs. The result was a dog similar to today's Labrador retriever, usually called a Lab.

These excellent hunting dogs made their way to England in the early 1800s. There, they became popular with sportsmen. The **breed** eventually died out in Newfoundland. Luckily, it continued to thrive in England. The **American Kennel Club (AKC)** registered the first Labs in 1917.

Families own Labs because they are easygoing and gentle. Labs love attention and always want to be included in family activities. They are smart and obedient. And, they love to swim and play fetch. Labs need a lot of exercise or they may become bored and cause mischief.

In 1991, the Lab became the most popular dog breed in the United States.

7

POODLES

Poodles are among the world's most popular dogs. That is not surprising. They are smart and eager to please. And, they make excellent watchdogs.

Most dogs have fur that grows and then falls out, or sheds. But like human hair, poodle coats grow long and need trimming. This means poodles shed less than most dogs. So, they are easier to have around people with allergies to dog fur.

Today's poodles originated in Germany during the 1500s. Poodles were first **bred** to help hunters locate and bring in wild **game** from water. Later, they became popular with European kings and queens.

Poodles arrived in the United States in the late 1800s. In 1887, the **AKC** recognized the breed. Today, poodles are among the AKC's top ten most popular dog breeds.

Poodles are **bred** in three sizes. The standard poodle is the largest and the most calm. The next smaller size is the miniature poodle. The toy poodle is the smallest.

Because of its intelligence, the poodle is one of the easiest breeds to train.

LABRADOODLE STORY

An Australian man named Wally Conron **bred** the first Labradoodles in 1989. Conron was trying to find a guide dog for a woman named Pat Blum. However, Blum needed a nonshedding dog because of her husband's allergies.

Conron bred a Labrador retriever with a standard poodle. One of the puppies, Sultan, did not upset Blum's husband's allergies. So, Sultan spent ten years as Blum's guide dog.

Most mother dogs are pregnant for about 63 days. Labradoodle puppies are born blind and deaf.

The Labradoodle's low-shedding coat was an attractive feature. And, its friendly, gentle disposition made it popular for work as a guide dog and a therapy dog. Soon, more people began **breeding** Labradoodles.

Together, poodles and Labs make a popular crossbreed, the Labradoodle!

LABRADOODLES

First-generation Labradoodles are **bred** from a female Lab and a male poodle. First-generation crossbreeding can eliminate many health problems.

Thanks to controlled breeding, there are multiple generations of Labradoodles today. These Labradoodles have both a mother and a father that are Labradoodles. They are athletic and graceful. They truly look like a breed of their own.

The **AKC** does not recognize the Labradoodle as a breed. Still, some Labradoodle breeders have put together breed standards.

Many breeders hope that one day the Labradoodle will be recognized worldwide as a breed.

BEHAVIOR

Labradoodle personalities reflect their Lab and poodle parents. They are sociable and friendly. And, they are extremely loyal to their families.

Labradoodles tend to be calmer and bark less than poodles. They are well behaved around other dogs and strangers.

Labradoodles have a lot of energy! They enjoy a daily on-leash walk and a chance to run free in a fenced-in area.

Just like Labs and poodles, Labradoodles are smart and easy to train. This makes them ideal guide dogs or therapy dogs.

Because Labradoodles are very intelligent, they need special care. Obedience training is a good idea, as is some activity each day. Like any smart dog, Labradoodles can get into trouble if they become bored.

Coats & Colors

Many Labradoodle **breeders** look for dogs that have either fleece or wool coats. Fleece coats are soft. They can be straight, wavy, or hang in loose, loopy spirals. Wool coats are thicker than fleece coats and feel like a soft, woolly sweater. Both types of coats should be four to six inches (10 to 15 cm) long.

Those long coats require care. Labradoodle owners should brush their dogs once a week. A couple of times a year, owners need to trim their Labradoodle's coat. Remember, Labradoodle hair is a lot like human hair. It keeps growing, so it needs to be trimmed.

Labradoodles can come in many colors. These include black, gold, apricot, red, cream, chocolate, and silver. Dogs that spend a lot of time outside may

have lighter-colored coats on top. This is from the sun. **Breeders** call this effect sunning.

A Labradoodle's coat should never be cut with clippers. Instead, the owner or the groomer should use scissors.

Sizes

Like poodles, Labradoodles come in three sizes. Each Labradoodle's size depends mostly on the size of the poodle it descends from. Standard, miniature, and toy poodles are used to **breed** Labradoodles.

The largest Labradoodles are the standard Labradoodles. They stand 22 to 26 inches (56 to 66 cm) tall. They weigh 55 to 88 pounds (25 to 40 kg).

Medium Labradoodles stand between 17 and 22 inches (43 and 56 cm) tall. They weigh 44 to 55 pounds (20 to 25 kg). Miniature Labradoodles stand just 13 to 17 inches (33 to 43 cm) tall. They weigh 22 to 44 pounds (10 to 20 kg).

There may be other sizes of Labradoodles. However, many **breeders** only recognize these three.

Guide dog work isn't just for larger Labradoodles. Miniature Labradoodles are perfect for assisting the elderly.

CARE

Labradoodles need at least one walk a day and lots of time with people. After all, both Labs and poodles enjoy being the center of attention. Labradoodles are no different.

Labradoodles also require regular visits to a veterinarian. As puppies, Labradoodles need vaccinations to prevent common canine diseases. Labradoodles should be **spayed** or **neutered** at the proper age if puppies are not desired.

Many Labradoodle **breeders** have tried to eliminate the most common health problems of both poodles and Labs. Both breeds tend to have hip and eye problems. In particular, Labs and poodles have a tendency to get an eye disease called prcd-PRA.

Labradoodle owners and their veterinarians should be on the lookout for such problems. With proper care and a balanced diet, a Labradoodle should be a loving part of its family for 12 to 14 years.

This active dog needs plenty of fresh water to drink and soft, clean bedding to nap on.

GLOSSARY

American Kennel Club (AKC) - an organization that studies and promotes interest in purebred dogs.

breed - a group of animals sharing the same appearance and characteristics. A breeder is a person who raises animals. Raising animals is often called breeding them.

family - a group that scientists use to classify similar plants or animals. It ranks above a genus and below an order.

game - wild animals hunted for food or sport.

neuter - to remove a male animal's reproductive organs.

purebred - an animal whose parents are both from the same breed.

spay - to remove a female animal's reproductive organs.

22

WEB SITES

To learn more about designer dogs, visit ABDO Publishing Company on the World Wide Web at **www.abdopublishing.com**. Web sites about designer dogs are featured on our Book Links page. These links are routinely monitored and updated to provide the most current information available.

23

INDEX